MISCHIEVOUS CATS

ADD

Illustrated by
Agnieszka Sikorska

Bloomsbury
Books

First published by Bloomsbury Books
an imprint of The Godfrey Cave Group
42 Bloomsbury Street
London WC1B 3QJ

ISBN 1-85471-658-1

Conceived and designed by Savitri Books Ltd
Printed and bound in Great Britain

The illustrations in this book are the work of Agnieszka Sikorska who is a Polish artist living in Gdansk. She specialises in restoration work and also teaches at the School of Art in Gdansk. She and her husband run an art gallery. They have two children and Agnieszka's other passion is cats.

A

Names & Addresses	*Telephone*

Names & Addresses	*Telephone*

Names & Addresses	Telephone

Names & Addresses	*Telephone*
Jack & Kath Berry. "Welwyn" Quantock View Bish Lyd	432275
Angie Beale. 48, George St.	337231.
Lyn Burgess. 1, Queensdown C.S.M.	442638.
Bus Station.	272033.
Chrissy Burgess. 21 Stoberry Ave. Wells. BA5.	

Names & Addresses	Telephone

Names & Addresses	*Telephone*

C

Names & Addresses	*Telephone*
Pam & Margaret Craft. "Ivydene", Gaston St, East Bergholt. Nr Colchester	
Syb. Climo. 24. Richmond Rd.	
Ethel Cornish. Bharaib, 17, Manor Rd. Alcombe.	01643. 705424.
Patsy & John Cozens 2. Colin Road.	274674.
Joan Crowley. 108, Galmington Rd.	289226.
Wendy & Bernard Coleman "Mallows" K.S.M. TA2 8HW.	451261.
Cattery.	337207

Names & Addresses	*Telephone*

Names & Addresses	Telephone

Names & Addresses	*Telephone*
Marilyn & John Dickenson, 35, Merlin Way East Grinstead Sussex.	R.H.19.3XG. 01342. 313451.

Names & Addresses	*Telephone*

Names & Addresses	*Telephone*

E

Names & Addresses	*Telephone*

Names & Addresses	*Telephone*

Names & Addresses	*Telephone*

F

Names & Addresses	*Telephone*

Names & Addresses	*Telephone*

Names & Addresses	Telephone

G

Names & Addresses	*Telephone*

Names & Addresses	*Telephone*

Names & Addresses	*Telephone*

H

Names & Addresses	*Telephone*

Names & Addresses	*Telephone*

Names & Addresses	*Telephone*

Names & Addresses	Telephone

Names & Addresses	Telephone

Names & Addresses	*Telephone*

Names & Addresses	Telephone

Names & Addresses	*Telephone*

Names & Addresses	Telephone

K

Names & Addresses	Telephone

Names & Addresses	Telephone

Names & Addresses	*Telephone*

Names & Addresses	*Telephone*

Names & Addresses	Telephone

Names & Addresses	*Telephone*

Names & Addresses	*Telephone*

Names & Addresses	*Telephone*

Names & Addresses	*Telephone*

N

Names & Addresses	*Telephone*

Names & Addresses	*Telephone*

Names & Addresses	*Telephone*

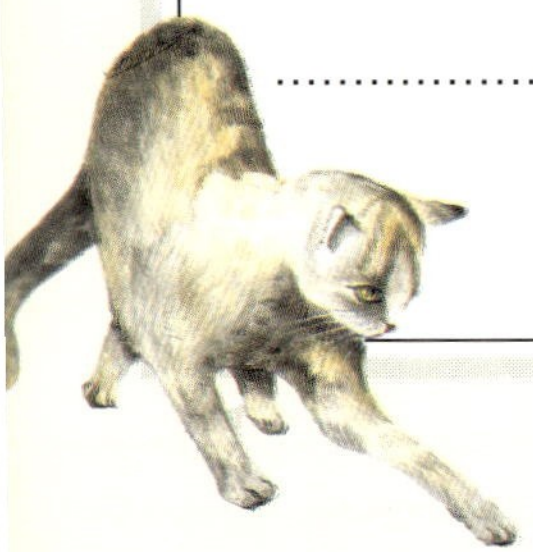

o

Names & Addresses	*Telephone*

Names & Addresses	*Telephone*

Names & Addresses	*Telephone*

Names & Addresses	*Telephone*

Names & Addresses	*Telephone*

Names & Addresses	*Telephone*

Q

Names & Addresses	*Telephone*

Names & Addresses	*Telephone*

Names & Addresses	Telephone

R

Names & Addresses	*Telephone*

Names & Addresses	*Telephone*

Names & Addresses	*Telephone*

S

Names & Addresses	*Telephone*

Names & Addresses	Telephone

Names & Addresses	Telephone

T

Names & Addresses	Telephone

Names & Addresses	Telephone

Names & Addresses	Telephone

U V

Names & Addresses	*Telephone*

Names & Addresses	*Telephone*

Names & Addresses	*Telephone*

WX

Names & Addresses	*Telephone*

Names & Addresses	*Telephone*

Names & Addresses	Telephone

Names & Addresses	*Telephone*